# THE IDEA ACCELERATOR

**KEN HUDSON** has a PhD in organisational creativity. His thesis explored the notion of 'designing a continuously creative organisation'.

Ken has also worked in senior roles for over 15 years in marketing, advertising and management consulting. He formed his own Speed Thinking business called The Speed Thinking Zone. Ken has worked with many leading brands, including Heinz, Wrigley, Colgate, Kellogg's, Unilever, Disney, DuPont and Nestlé. He is the author of *The Idea Generator* (Allen & Unwin, 2007).

Ken can be contacted at **www.thespeedthinkingzone.com**

# THE IDEA ACCELERATOR

## How to solve problems faster using **Speed Thinking**

# KEN HUDSON

ALLEN&UNWIN

First published in 2008

Allen & Unwin
83 Alexander Street
Crows Nest NSW 2065
Australia
Phone:      (61 2) 8425 0100
Fax:        (61 2) 9906 2218
Email:      info@allenandunwin.com
Web:        www.allenandunwin.com

National Library of Australia
Cataloguing-in-Publication entry:

Hudson, Ken.
    The idea accelerator : how to solve problems faster using speed thinking.

    Bibliography.
    ISBN: 978 1 74175 488 9 (pbk.)

    Problem solving.
    Creative thinking.
    Creative ability in business.

650.1

Internal design by Kirby Stalgis
Set in 10/14 pt Berling by Bookhouse, Sydney
Printed in Australia by McPherson's Printing Group

10 9 8 7 6 5 4 3 2 1

# CONTENTS

In memory of Ray O'Neill, a man of big dreams and Gloria O'Neill, a remarkable and courageous woman.

This book is dedicated to Margot, Molly and Charlotte who in their own way make my heart beat faster.

I would also like to thank my publisher Ian Bowring for supporting the concept and to my editors Karen Gee and Angela Handley for making this book infinitely better.

A special thank you to my agent Carolyn Crowther for her unbridled enthusiasm.

# INTRODUCTION

Everywhere I go I hear the same lament—if only I had more time. Time, not money, has become our most precious resource. Not only is there less time in the day but there is always more to do. And the pace of life seems to be increasing. That weekend away at the beach always seems to beckon but we never quite make it.

The premise of this book is that limited time is the new reality for most people. It is the rule rather than the exception. It is not a question of working harder—most people are already stretched to the limit. Nor is it enough to be a better time manager. We need a new approach and that is what this book is all about.

Our new priority should be to improve the productivity of our thinking—to generate greater results in a shorter period of time. Until now, we have concentrated on improving the return on physical assets (e.g. machinery). Increasingly, the work of the future will be conceptual rather than physical. We all must improve our thinking muscle. Immediate results require faster, better thinking.

In a broadband-paced world the speed with which we process information, create new solutions and make decisions has to accelerate. To adapt to this new reality requires an entirely new style that I have called Speed Thinking. This type of thinking, however, does not negate the importance of the more conscious, deliberate, and reflective approach. Rather, it complements it, much like Speed Chess resembles the original but has its own distinct rules and flavour.

Fortunately we are very good at what Malcolm Gladwell (among others) calls rapid cognition.[1] He calls it the 'universal ability of our unconscious to find patterns in situations and behaviour based on very narrow slices of experiences'. As it turns out we are also very adept at using our intuition to make fast decisions under extreme pressure.[2] So the idea of Speed Thinking has been around for a while, but what we have lacked is a tool kit to help us improve upon this ability. That is what this book aims to give you.

In my workshops I have found that accelerated thinking allows you to access, almost at will, your amazing, creative mental ability. Timothy D. Wilson calls this our Adaptive Unconscious, which plays a major executive role in gathering information, interpreting and evaluating it. It also sets goals in motion quickly and efficiently.[3]

I stumbled upon this universal ability almost by accident. To create some urgency and drama in my creative workshops I kept reducing the amount of time I gave participants to solve a problem.

But a strange thing happened: the less time I gave people, the more ideas they produced and, as importantly, the originality of the ideas became more pronounced. In turn, participants were amazed at what they could produce in such a small period of time.

# INTRODUCTION

## Bypassing your two judges

In reflecting on why people can become more creative in a shorter period of time I came to the conclusion that it is because we all have what I call two judges—one internal, the other external. It is these judges that suppress our natural creative instincts.

The internal judge is our own (often) critical voice that warns us our ideas may not be very good and that we are not creative. This idea is reflected in the work of W. Timothy Gallwey, who postulated that in sport and life we maintain a constant dialogue between what he calls Self 1 (the commentator) and Self 2 (the doer).[4] Self 1 not only gives instructions to Self 2 but criticises past errors, warns of possible future ones and harangues whenever there is a mistake. I found this also resonated with my experience. We are often the greatest critic of our own ideas. Paradoxically, if we are only given a limited amount of time we are forced to ignore our Self 1 and just get our big, beautiful ideas out.

The other judge is the external one. It relates to our friends, peers, colleagues and bosses. We are often so worried by what they might say or how critical they can be that we suppress our unconscious imagination and intuition. This often leads to safe, incremental ideas and solutions. Sports people, for example, know that worrying how others might judge their performance can create a negative spiral. As the Yankees' third baseman and baseball's highest paid player, Alex Rodriguez responded when trying to explain his amazing form: 'I'm just trying to have as much fun as I can and really not care about what people are thinking or saying.'[5] With the Speed Thinking approach you literally have no time to worry about what anyone else thinks. You are too busy creating.

## The benefits of Speed Thinking

In the many workshops I have run using the tools in this book participants have mentioned the benefits listed below. Their usual response after a period of intense creativity is 'Where did that come from?'

### *People are more focused*

When people are given only a short time to develop a new range of ideas they become incredibly focused. There is a short burst of creative energy, and people become absorbed in the here and now, which can often lead to a circuit-breaking solution.

### *The approach leads to greater action*

Paradoxically, giving people too much time to think can lead to paralysis by analysis. Providing a short window of time sometimes short-circuits this and creates more energy and action.

### *The big elephants are tackled*

This is a surprising result. I have observed that giving people less time to tackle an issue means they have to address the large issues rather than dwell on the periphery. This means that meetings are often more productive and effective in half the time.

### *The number of ideas is increased*

The Speed Thinking approach emphasises working from the individual up to the group. This means, for example, that if ten people can create nine ideas each in 120 seconds then you have 90 ideas in the time taken to eat a chocolate bar.

*It can have a positive effect on your mood*

Recent research by Emily Pronin and Daniel Wegner suggests that the very process of thinking faster almost regardless of the content could improve the way you feel.[6]

*Speed Thinking can be used by an individual or a group*

The Speed Thinking tool kit can be used with great effect by individuals, people working together and/or in a group.

*The learning experience is profound*

Just like the *One Minute Manager* technique, people can undergo an important learning experience because the tools are so practical and the effect is immediate.[7]

## The structure of Speed Thinking

This book outlines 60 Speed Thinking tools. There are six chapters with ten tools in each chapter. Each tool is described on one page and on the opposite page is an application or example of the tool. There are chapters on how you can use the tools when working alone, when working with a partner or group and how to enhance, evaluate and action ideas working at speed. The Conclusion then addresses some of the most commonly asked questions about this type of thinking.

The Speed Thinking tools can be learned by anyone, at any level, regardless of their role or industry. You do not need a university education to use this book. The tools are practical and have been tested over a number of years. I have found, for example, that the optimum time to solve a problem using this approach is 120 seconds with an ideal target of nine responses. You may not reach this initially but with practice and by using the tools in this book you can reach this goal.

## Who this book is written for

This book will be of tremendous value to leaders, managers, small business owners, consultants, coaches and university students. Most of the examples are more business oriented but the tools can be used for any application.

# THE IDEA ACCELERATOR

'Speed will help you bypass your
Censor.'

Mark Bryan, Julia Cameron and Catherine Allen,
*The Artist's Way at Work*

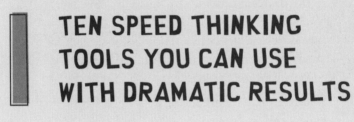

# TEN SPEED THINKING TOOLS YOU CAN USE WITH DRAMATIC RESULTS

# The 120-second challenge

Whatever problem you are working on, try to crystallise it into one sentence or at most a paragraph.

Say the problem out loud to yourself. Then say 'start' or 'go' and give yourself 120 seconds to come up with as many different solutions or new ideas as you can. You should aim for at least nine. Just use a key word or an image to capture the idea.

The emphasis is on producing as many different solutions to the problem as you can. You will find you will not have time to evaluate if you want to get nine ideas down on paper.

The simple process of concentrating on increasing the number of ideas will decrease your rational, judging mind and enable you to access your intuition and imagination.

An extension of this tool is to think of nine radical ideas in 120 seconds. Do not be safe or incremental in your responses.

## Application

**The challenge:** *How can I ensure I arrive on time to all my appointments?*

As quickly as you can in the next 120 seconds try to write down at least nine ways of meeting the above challenge—below is an example.

| | | |
|---|---|---|
| **1** Put watch forward | **2** Leave earlier | **3** Only schedule morning meetings |
| **4** Use a stop watch | **5** Have a watch on each hand | **6** Keep a clock in every room |
| **7** Send warnings to myself | **8** Have friends warn me | **9** Change other people's watches |

Now select and test the best ones.

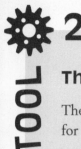

**TOOL 2**

## The two-hourly re-challenge

The aim with this tool is to concentrate on one problem for the entire day.

Clarify the problem at the start of the day and take up the 120-second challenge, aiming to develop at least nine responses. Be sure to record the results.

Then move on to your other work. In two hours return to the original problem.

Allow yourself another 120 seconds to develop a new set of solutions.

There is only one rule: you must not repeat an idea.

This cycle should be repeated every two hours until you have at least 40 different ideas.

Then select the best ideas and try to test these quickly, easily and simply.

## Application

Focus on one problem for the entire day. Develop five possible solutions every two hours. At the end of the day select the most original response and test it.

The problem: _____

Date: _____

**First two hours**
1
2
3
4
5

**Second two hours**
1
2
3
4
5

**Third two hours**
1
2
3
4
5

**Fourth two hours**
1
2
3
4
5

## Breathe in—breathe out

Concentrate all your mental energy on a specific problem.

Now close your eyes and really focus on your breath. Slow your breathing down and feel your chest move in and out.

Take two big breaths and open your eyes before you start.

On the third exhalation try to think of a new solution. Just write down one key thought.

From then on try to create a new idea with every second exhalation.

Try to do this for ten breaths and you will have five new ideas. This is also a very good tool to use with a partner as you take it in turns to solve a problem.

The important point with this exercise is for the breath to be calm and long, not shallow and short. This exercise will help to clear your mind and will often lower your stress levels.

## Application

*The challenge:* _____

| Breath one: | Key thought: |
| Breath two: | Key thought: |
| Breath three: | Key thought: |
| Breath four: | Key thought: |
| Breath five: | Key thought: |

Now select the best option and test it.

## The Richard Branson boost

The concept behind this tool is for you to imagine yourself as someone who is renowned for their creativity or entrepreneurship.

Let's select Sir Richard Branson as an example, the founder of the Virgin group of companies. Select a problem and in 120 seconds you have to imagine how he might solve the problem. Remember you need at least nine solutions.

The next time you do this you can imagine how another person might solve the problem: it could be your boss, Oprah Winfrey or Albert Einstein.

Then try to play around with your ideas. Combine ideas number three and five, for instance, to create an even bigger idea. Or focus on developing one option selected at random, e.g. idea number seven.

## Application

*The challenge:* How can I kick-start my career?

As quickly as you can in the next 120 seconds imagine Richard Branson as your coach. What would he advise? Here are some sample ideas.

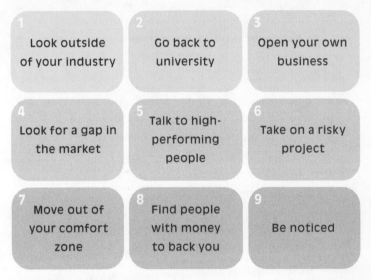

| 1 | 2 | 3 |
|---|---|---|
| Look outside of your industry | Go back to university | Open your own business |
| 4 | 5 | 6 |
| Look for a gap in the market | Talk to high-performing people | Take on a risky project |
| 7 | 8 | 9 |
| Move out of your comfort zone | Find people with money to back you | Be noticed |

Now select the best option and test it.

# 5

## A letter a day

The aim in this tool is to use a letter of the alphabet to help you solve a problem.

Make Monday the letter 'A' day, Tuesday the letter 'B' day, and so on.[1]

After defining the problem try to think of as many different ways you can solve it using the letter 'A' in the next 120 seconds.

This is a very good tool to use when you are facing a particularly difficult problem and you feel stuck. It is also a good tool to use with a partner. Both work on the same problem for 120 seconds but you use the letter 'A', for example, and your partner must use the letter 'B'. The results may surprise you both.

## Application

**The challenge:** *How can I better manage my work–life balance?*

As quickly as you can in the next 120 seconds try to create at least nine different possibilities using the letter 'A'.

| | | |
|---|---|---|
| 1 Argue with my boss when he/she is making unfair demands | 2 Acknowledge others who are trying to lead a more balanced life | 3 Arrange meetings while commuting |
| 4 Apple a day (i.e. watch my diet) | 5 Apply time management principles | 6 Always say no to weekend work |
| 7 Assign work to others | 8 Applaud (i.e. go and watch sport/live music) | 9 Appreciate (i.e. time with family) |

Now select the best option and test it.

**TOOL**

**6**

## The 60-second challenge

As you practise these tools you will become quicker and quicker.

After becoming proficient at the 120-second challenge try to decrease the time allowed for generating your nine ideas to 60 seconds.

Then move to 45 seconds.

If you find you can develop nine ideas in 45 seconds, go back to two minutes just as a test: it will seem like an eternity.

You will not have time to record a complete idea so just capture the essence of the idea in a key word or image.

## Application

*The challenge: How can I enjoy work more?*

As quickly as you can in the next 60 seconds try to develop at least nine different possible ideas, as in the example below.

Now select a couple and test them.

**7**

**TOOL**

## The five senses

We all have five senses:

- sight
- sound
- touch
- smell
- taste.

Yet in most circumstances we tend to be dominated by the sense of sight.

Try using one of your other senses. If you are designing a new product, for example, or want to enhance a customer experience consider the sense of smell. Can you imagine the smell of a South American jungle or a field in spring? How can you apply this aroma in your business?

For the next 120 seconds try to use one of your senses to add something new to your product or service. Go for as many different responses as you can imagine.

## Application

*The challenge:* To develop a new kids breakfast cereal.

Imagine experiencing the world as a kid. What do you see, hear, touch, taste and smell?

**Sight only:**

> **Key thoughts:**
> e.g. rainbow colours

**Sound only:**

> **Key thoughts:**
> e.g. the noises of the playground

**Touch only:**

> **Key thoughts:**
> e.g. make it bumpy

**Taste only:**

> **Key thoughts:**
> e.g. explodes in the mouth

**Smell only:**

> **Key thoughts:**
> e.g. the fresh grass in the park

## 'Thank you'

With this tool try to develop new ways that the customer will say 'thank you' because your product or service is so good or you have solved a problem for them in a new and innovative way.

For example, being able to swap your investments around at will so that you always have the highest return might be something for which the customer will feel thankful. Or another might be if you lose your credit card and the company can have a new one to you within an hour.

Select a product or new business idea and set yourself the task of developing at least nine reasons for which a customer might say 'thank you'. This will help put you in the customer's shoes and therefore develop ideas based on their expectations.

An extension of this idea is to develop in 120 seconds at least nine reasons for which an employee, partner or supplier might say 'thank you'.

## Application

**The challenge:** *Recall the service you receive at a bank—what are nine reasons for which the customer might say 'thank you'?*

Only take 120 seconds to complete the spaces below.

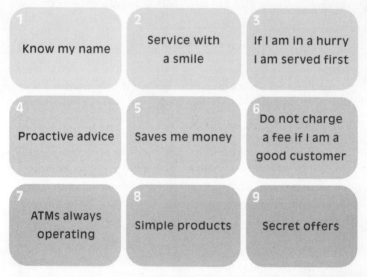

Once you have completed this exercise, select one of the options at random and spend another 120 seconds on developing the raw idea. Or try combining a number of these to develop a bigger idea.

**TOOL 9**

## Rapid drawing

Sometimes the best way to create a new solution or set of ideas is to draw them. This helps you to escape our language-based thinking system. It is true that a picture can replace a thousand words.

First define the problem. Then in the next 120 seconds draw the problem. Remember you only have 120 seconds so your drawing ability is not the issue. Draw something that might represent the problem. For example, if you want to represent a customer service issue you could draw a bird in a cage.

In the following 120 seconds draw a few possible solutions. Then work out what the images are trying to convey and how to make it happen.

This is also a very good exercise to do with a group as you can end up with a range of very different images or drawings. It is also an effective tool when you are dealing with a sensitive political issue as emotions can often be more richly expressed in images than words.

## Application

*Define the problem:* _____

| Draw the problem in 120 seconds | Draw the solution in 120 seconds |
|---|---|
| | |

| | Draw another solution in 120 seconds |
|---|---|
| | |

**10**

**TOOL**

## Express emotions

Your emotions provide the pathway to your imagination. This tool encourages you to harness your emotions to solve problems in a new way.

Write down as many different emotions as you can think of in the next 120 seconds. For example: joy, sadness, love, happiness, fear, apathy etc.

Then select one of these at random, say the fourth one, to solve a problem at hand (see the example opposite).

You will be amazed at how quickly you can connect an emotion to the problem. In fact, the more unrelated the emotion to the problem the better.

## Application

*The challenge:* How can I improve team spirit among the people in my department?

In the next 120 seconds write down as many different emotions as you can think of. Then select one emotion at random e.g. happiness. Develop at least nine ways happiness can help you address the challenge above.

| | | |
|---|---|---|
| **1** Don't employ cynical people | **2** Avoid unhappy people | **3** Do more things that the group cares about |
| **4** Learn some good jokes | **5** Involve new employees | **6** Say 'thank you' more often |
| **7** Start each meeting with a joke | **8** Encourage social events | **9** Play sport together |

'*Feel confident that the first option you think of will usually be a good one.*'

Gary Klein, **The Power of Intuition**

# 2 TEN SPEED THINKING TOOLS TO USE WHEN WORKING WITH A COLLEAGUE

# 1

## The joint 120-second challenge

This is an ideal starting tool when you are working with a partner or colleague.

First, agree on a joint problem.

Each person has 120 seconds to create at least nine new solutions. This should be done independently.

Then discuss your new ideas with each other. The best ideas should be evaluated and the top three decided upon.

Then develop at least nine ways you can build the top idea into a stronger one. Try doing this together.

Once you have built a strong concept, move on to the next high priority idea.

## Application

*The joint challenge:* How can we improve our results at work?

Work by yourself, and as quickly as you can in the next 120 seconds write down at least nine ways of meeting the above challenge. Then discuss and agree on the best ideas and work these up using the same process. Try to combine thoughts e.g. take the number two and combine with number seven to build an even bigger idea.

| 1 | 2 | 3 |
|---|---|---|
| Do more work | Hire a coach | Talk to a mentor |

| 4 | 5 | 6 |
|---|---|---|
| Try new things | Share what we learn | Give up work we do not enjoy |

| 7 | 8 | 9 |
|---|---|---|
| Ask more questions | Read related topics | Have lunch with the top performers |

# 2

## On a deadline—write a headline

Agree upon the problem with your partner, e.g. how can we encourage speed thinking throughout the organisation?

One person has to imagine themselves as an online reporter who has been given 120 seconds to write a headline on the new solution to your problem.

For example: If the problem is to encourage more people to think more quickly a possible headline might be 'Exciting News—IBM has employees who can think faster than its computers'.

Once the first person has written a number of headlines the second person must develop the headline into a more complete story. Try to do this quickly just using bullet points.

After you have developed the first headline and story, swap roles. Try to repeat three times each.

## Application

*The joint challenge:* To ensure airlines leave on time.

| | |
|---|---|
| **Headline 1:** 'Frequent Flyers Soar' | **Key story highlights:** Frequent Flyers receive bonus points if they arrive early. |
| **Headline 2** | **Key story highlights:** |
| **Headline 3** | **Key story highlights:** |

**TOOL 3**

## The 120-second interview

This tool builds upon the previous one. The aim in this tool is for each person to interview the other in 120 seconds about the problem.

First, agree upon the problem.

The clock then starts and both people independently write down as many different or unusual questions as they can think of about the problem itself.

They then take it in turns to interview one another.

Take note of the questions that you cannot answer and/or those questions that are original—these might be an area to really focus on.

## Application

*The joint challenge:* To discover what is behind the success of many small businesses.

| | |
|---|---|
| **Your questions:** | **Possible interview questions:** <br>• Can anyone run a successful small business? <br>• What did you do that didn't work? <br>• If you had your time over again what would you do differently? |
| **Your partner's questions:** | **Possible interview questions:** <br>• How important is it to have your family behind you? <br>• How do you create your new ideas? <br>• Do you have time for your family? |
| **What questions did you struggle with?** | |

## TOOL 4

## Three big ideas

This tool is a fun way to develop some breakthrough ideas. The starting point is to have each person try to imagine the biggest joint goal that both of you could achieve in the next 12 months. For example, if both your work performances have been rated in the average range how can you deliver a top 10 per cent rating in the next review?

Each person is then given 120 seconds to develop three big (*really* big) ideas. Each of you works independently and then you present your ideas to each other.

Together you then enhance each other's big ideas and work on one big idea for 120 seconds. When you have finished you will have six bold, developed concepts.

## Application

*The joint challenge:* How can we double our business?

| Big idea 1: e.g. Try to partner with other companies | Ways to develop this idea: • Talk to your suppliers • Talk to your partners • Research other players |
|---|---|
| Big idea 2: | Ways to develop this idea: |
| Big idea 3: | Ways to develop this idea: |

**5**

**TOOL**

## The 'moment of truth' narrative

Every customer considering purchasing a product or service has a 'moment of truth', the exact moment when they must decide one way or another whether to buy or not.

For this tool, each of you has 120 seconds to act out this moment of truth narrative with your partner. You must make your exact emotions and thought processes explicit. You should provide a running commentary to the other person of what is going on in your mind. Close your eyes so that you put the other person's physical presence out of your mind.

The other person writes down the narrative or internal conversation, as they perceive it to be. After 120 seconds you swap roles and repeat the exercise.

After this, you then discuss the common elements and the real hot buttons you can influence and which product is better or worse than others.

## Application

*The joint challenge:* How can we improve sales of our mobile phones?

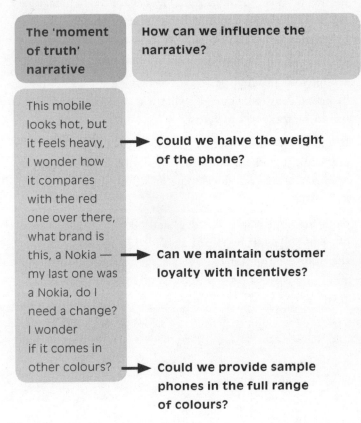

| The 'moment of truth' narrative | How can we influence the narrative? |
|---|---|
| This mobile looks hot, but it feels heavy, I wonder how it compares with the red one over there, what brand is this, a Nokia — my last one was a Nokia, do I need a change? I wonder if it comes in other colours? | **Could we halve the weight of the phone?**<br><br>**Can we maintain customer loyalty with incentives?**<br><br>**Could we provide sample phones in the full range of colours?** |

## TOOL 6

## The Godfather test

In the original *Godfather* movie one of the characters famously remarked to another character that he would make them an offer too good to refuse.

This simple technique represents a very effective way of selling your product or service or coming up with a new business idea. Ask yourself, what is a customer offer that would be too good to refuse?

If you are working with a partner, select a problem or opportunity you are both interested in. Each person then spends 120 seconds developing an offer that is too good to refuse.

Compare your respective ideas and take the best features of each. Finish off by taking another 120 seconds to make the offer even better.

## Application

*The joint challenge:* To sell our house at the highest price in the shortest possible time.

Work by yourself. As quickly as you can in the next 120 seconds write down at least nine ways to elicit an offer that is too good to refuse. Then discuss your ideas and develop a 'best of' offer that should be irresistible.

| | | |
|---|---|---|
| **1** Have 24-hour viewings, 7 days a week | **2** Do your own mail-drop | **3** Offer agent a $20k bonus if they achieve a certain price |
| **4** Arrange your own PR | **5** Throw in the car if the house sells by a certain time | **6** The price includes all the furniture |
| **7** Offer to clean the place for the next 12 months | **8** Add $20k worth of building repairs | **9** Pay for an architect to work with the new buyers |

**TOOL 7**

## Overcoming barriers

Sometimes the process of identifying and writing down the barriers that you are facing can lead to more productive actions.

Try this exercise: select one of the following statements, then in the next 120 seconds write down as many barriers to it that you can think of. Have your partner do the same.

*The biggest barriers to my success at work are…*

*The biggest barriers to me growing the business are…*

*The biggest barriers stopping me from losing weight are…*

Select one of the barriers from your partner's list and they will select one from yours.

Spend another 120 seconds thinking of ways to overcome each other's barrier.

## Application

***The joint challenge:*** *To discover what is stopping me losing weight.*

Work by yourself. As quickly as you can in the next 120 seconds write down at least nine barriers that are stopping you meeting the above challenge.

Then discuss together how to tackle some of these barriers and draw up an action plan to overcome them.

## Two minute risk-taking

Many people in life avoid taking any type of risk. But taking risks in life and work can be rewarding and can ensure that you will continue to grow.

In the next 120 seconds write down some risks that you can take this week. Ask your partner to do the same.

For example, it could be the risk of asking a seemingly naïve question or wearing something inappropriate when you go out. The risks do not have to be big risks; they can be everyday ones.

Taking some form of risk, however small, keeps us alive and young at heart.

## Application

**The joint challenge:** *To identify nine small risks we can take this week.*

Each person should list the risks they might consider taking this week. Select one risk from each other's list and then spend another 120 seconds helping one another to accept that risk. Or perhaps minimise it so that following through with the risk-taking action does not cripple you with fear.

| | | |
|---|---|---|
| 1 **Go to a movie by myself** | 2 **Read a fiction book** | 3 **Ask the first question in a meeting** |
| 4 **Don't drink when I go to a party** | 5 **Ask someone for help** | 6 **Cook a new meal** |
| 7 **Drive a new way to work** | 8 **Wear a fake tattoo for a day** | 9 **Buy a CD by an unknown artist** |

**TOOL 9**

## Nine things I hate about my job

This is a very effective and practical way of designing a new job and trying to reduce the things that annoy you.

The idea behind this tool is that sometimes our work causes us stress but we are not aware of why this might be the case. If we can make some of the reasons explicit then we can design a way of reducing their effect or, better still, eliminate them.

The other benefit of this exercise is that once you make a list of what really annoys you some of these activities you are not so keen on don't seem quite so bad.

# Application

***The joint challenge:*** *How can we identify the things that annoy us and try to reduce these?*

Work by yourself and quickly list at least nine things about your job that annoy you. Select one of the items from each other's list or perhaps find something you both do not like and try to solve it together. Discuss nine ways to solve it in the next 120 seconds. For example, many of the tools in this book can help you cope better with tight deadlines.

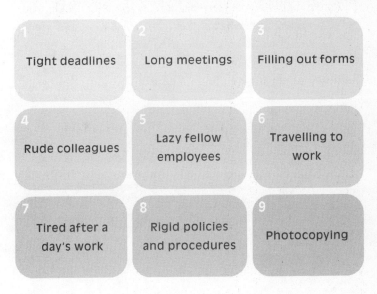

| 1 Tight deadlines | 2 Long meetings | 3 Filling out forms |
| --- | --- | --- |
| 4 Rude colleagues | 5 Lazy fellow employees | 6 Travelling to work |
| 7 Tired after a day's work | 8 Rigid policies and procedures | 9 Photocopying |

**10**

## Nine things I feel passionate about

What do you feel really passionate about in life? It could be riding a horse, playing golf or spending time playing with the kids. Whatever it is, try writing down nine examples in the next 120 seconds.

Ask your partner to do the same.

Identifying what you feel passionate about will help you really understand what makes you feel happy and alive. We all tend to be more enthused and often do a better job when we are working on activities that we care about most.

## Application

***The joint challenge:*** *To find out what we both feel most passionate about in our life.*

Working individually, write down at least nine things you feel passionate about as quickly as you can in the next 120 seconds. Then discuss your lists. Select one at random from both lists and see how you can factor this more into your life, or even make a living from it.

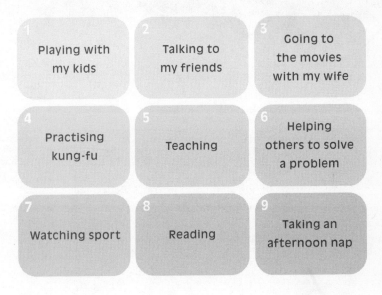

| 1 Playing with my kids | 2 Talking to my friends | 3 Going to the movies with my wife |
| 4 Practising kung-fu | 5 Teaching | 6 Helping others to solve a problem |
| 7 Watching sport | 8 Reading | 9 Taking an afternoon nap |

'*None of us is as smart as all of us.*'

Warren Bennis and Patricia Ward Biederman,
*Organizing Genius*

# 3 TEN SPEED THINKING TOOLS TO USE WHEN WORKING IN A GROUP

**TOOL 1**

## The 120-second group contest

Select a problem that the group or team should focus on. Be sure that everyone understands the problem.

Then set a challenge for every participant to come up with as many different solutions to the problem as they possibly can in the next 120 seconds.

Ask those with nine or more possible solutions to come out the front and compete with others in the group. They should work on the same problem but must not repeat any of their ideas. In the end you will have a winner and literally loads of ideas.

At the end of this exercise ask people to communicate their top three solutions but hand in all their solutions to the team leader.

This task can also be completed online.

## Application

*The group challenge:* How can we make groups more effective?

| | | |
|---|---|---|
| **1** Have smaller groups | **2** Form groups based on passion | **3** Include new people |
| **4** Develop a big goal | **5** Measure results | **6** Celebrate |
| **7** Study other groups | **8** Have fun | **9** Form a 30-day team only |

**TOOL**

# 2

## Idea ping-pong

The aim with this tool is to quickly bounce ideas back and forth with a partner or between small groups—much like ping-pong. The aim is to continually build on an initial idea and make it better.

Divide the larger group up into two smaller groups. Agree upon the problem then allocate one team to develop at least one big new idea in 120 seconds.

This becomes a starting point which the next team must build on. Each team has 60 seconds to add something powerful to the original idea.

The initial team should then add something further to the idea. This process goes back and forth five times. At the end of this period both groups can decide whether the end product is a fantastic idea.

This tool is a very good way to have two groups building on each other's ideas.

## Application

*The group challenge:* How can we raise money while enjoying ourselves?

**Group 1**

Let's go to the beach.

**Group 2**

What about a café on the beach?

We could have a surfing contest.

We could sponsor a contest and try to raise money.

The money raised could be donated to the surf-lifesaving club.

We could play Beach Boys music.

We could have a 'wildest beach dress' competition.

TOOL

## Catch a ball

This is a fun exercise that builds on the previous tool (idea ping-pong) and generates ideas very quickly in a group situation.

First, agree upon a problem that the group must solve. Then divide the group into a number of teams of, say, five or six people per team. These teams should then pair off and stand opposite each other, a few metres apart.

One person starts by throwing a ball to a member of the opposite team. They must catch the ball and then add one new idea or possible solution to the problem at hand. They should do this quickly and then throw the ball to another person on the other team. This person adds a new idea as they catch the ball. The ball goes back and forth until one team wins (if you drop the ball, cannot think of an idea immediately or throw a bad pass you are out).

Another team records the ideas.

People are always amazed at their responses when doing this exercise. Because you have to concentrate on the ball and think quickly you have no time to filter or censor your ideas. Your imagination is fully engaged and can create new ideas at will.

## Application

***The group challenge:*** *How can we improve our ability to remember someone's name?*

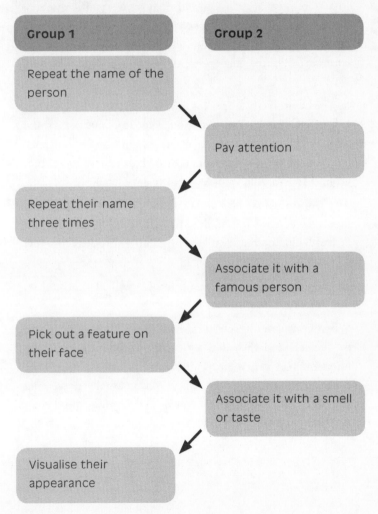

**Group 1**

Repeat the name of the person

**Group 2**

Pay attention

Repeat their name three times

Associate it with a famous person

Pick out a feature on their face

Associate it with a smell or taste

Visualise their appearance

## Mind map at speed

I have found that using a mind map is a very effective tool to create and capture ideas quickly. It is a simple tool developed by Tony Buzan which can also be used to summarise notes and present information in a visual way.[1]

My favourite way of using a mind map is to start with the individual and then engage the group. To construct a mind map, simply place the problem in the middle of your page and as possible solutions emerge you place these in bubbles around the middle bubble (i.e. the problem).

The group then decides upon a single problem. Each person is asked to create a mind map to try to resolve the problem at hand. Try to create at least nine different ideas in a few minutes.

Each individual should then number each of the bubbles outside the core problem bubble.

When completed, each mind map is passed to the person on the left and they add a new thought or build on the mind map before them. This process should be repeated around six times with the time given gradually decreasing from 120 seconds to 30 seconds. The original mind map is then returned to its owner.

## Application

***The group challenge:*** *How can we improve our business consulting practice?*

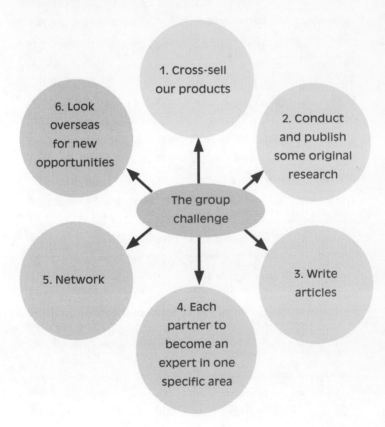

# 5

## Express image

When solving a problem it is often easier to use an image rather than words or sentences. This is because images can often better convey emotion and more sensitive political issues can be uncovered.

For example, consider the problem of how to improve the performance of a specific supplier. Ask each person to draw as many different images they can imagine in the next 120 seconds that might provide a clue to addressing this problem e.g. someone might have an image of the supplier falling off a cliff.

Then place these up on a wall and discuss what each image means to each member of the group and how it might provide a new solution to the problem at hand. Another option is to have a range of say 30 random images collected from the internet (e.g. a frog, a plane, a traffic jam etc.). Ask people to select an image as quickly as they can and be ready to discuss with the group how they feel it relates to the problem. You will be amazed at the variety of responses and images selected.

Another variation is to send out the problem beforehand to all group members and ask them to bring along at least one image that might shed light on a new array of solutions.

## Application

*The group challenge:* How can we improve the performance of a supplier?

**Image 1**

**What insight might this image provide?**
- An unhappy supplier
- Making no money
- Sees no future

**Image 2**

**What insight might this image provide?**

**Image 3**

**What insight might this image provide?**

**TOOL**

# 6

## The three roles

In trying to solve a problem or create a new concept there are often three different roles in any group.

The first role is to create an initial idea. The second one is to enhance the initial idea. Finally there is the evaluating role. Remember these are roles, not descriptions of people.

These roles can be practised in a group. Divide the larger group into groups of three.

Allocate one person to each of the three roles:
- the idea originator
- the enhancer
- the evaluator.

The exercise starts when each group decides upon a problem.

The originator must come up with at least three big ideas to solve the problem in 120 seconds. The enhancer must then build on each of these ideas in the next 120 seconds and the evaluator must then decide which idea is the best and give the reasons why.

The group members then swap roles and work on another problem. The advantage of this process is that everyone becomes better at each role. In addition, people who are often critical must try to create new ideas and hence have a new appreciation of how fragile the creative process can be.

## Application

*The group challenge:* How can we make our department more effective?

| Role 1: The originator (to create new ideas) | 1. Restructure the department. 2. Study other high-performing departments. 3. Merge the department with others. |
|---|---|
| Role 2: The enhancer (to build on the initial ideas) | 1. Structure the department from the customer perspective. 2. Study a department of similar size. 3. Create super departments and reduce middle management. |
| Role 3: The evaluator (to decide on the best approach) | Option number two might be the best; finding out what makes other high-performing departments tick might save a lot of time and energy, and stretch people. |

**TOOL**

## Three pieces of music

This is an amazing and very different speed thinking tool to use with a group.

The group is given a problem. They are then played one piece of music for 120 seconds. It could be Beethoven or Elton John—it does not matter. Each person is then asked for three big ideas or solutions to the problem that came into their consciousness as a result of listening to this particular piece of music.

Still working on the same problem, the group is then given another quite different piece of music and asked to create another three ideas or solutions inspired by this new music.

Finally, a third piece of music is played and the group is asked to develop three more solutions to the problem at hand.

After this, each person discusses their nine ideas with a smaller group. This smaller group decides on the two best ideas and presents these to the larger group, but all ideas are captured.

## Application

*The group challenge:* How can we reduce the friction in our group?

| **Music piece 1**<br>e.g. Mozart | Play some stirring music in the background when the group meets. |
| --- | --- |
| **Music piece 2**<br>e.g. Madonna | Reinvent the name of the group every year. |
| **Music piece 3**<br>e.g. hip-hop | Invite all group members to a nightclub. |

## The competitor's next 12 months

Much time is spent in business trying to understand the competition.

I have found that much of this discussion is based on what the competition has done rather than what they might do in the future.

To anticipate the competitor's likely moves requires imagination and intuition. This is why the Speed Thinking tools outlined in this book are ideal.

If you have a number of competitors split the group into smaller groups and ask each group to focus on one competitor. Have each person work by themselves and ask them to anticipate at least nine competitor's actions in the next 120 seconds.

Then have the group discuss the various ideas from each person and agree on the three that are the most likely to succeed. Develop a proactive strategy to gain the upper hand.

## Application

**The group challenge:** *To anticipate the actions of our primary competitor in the next 12 months.*

In the next 120 seconds have all group members outline what the main competitor might do in the next 12 months, as below.

Discuss how you might respond to these anticipated actions.

## TOOL 9

# The lunch-time safari

One of the best ways to think more productively is to use the time you already have for other activities to think more creatively or solve a difficult problem.

For example, if you are working with a group and you stop for a lunch break try challenging everyone to create three new big ideas before lunch is finished.

My suggestion is that each person is allocated a partner at random and they are given, say, $20 to buy each other lunch and hunt for ideas together.

This exercise works extremely well if you randomly allocate each pair three stores or places to visit during lunch. This is exactly what happened in one of my workshops when a pair stopped and watched a street performer—their insight from watching her engage the crowd was that their advertising was too grey and pedestrian by comparison and needed to be changed.

The other advantage of this approach is that you can pair up people who do not normally work together, which can lead to increased team morale and a better understanding of each other's perspectives.

## Application

*The group challenge:* How can we improve the shopping experience for our customers?

| McDonalds | e.g. Do we have staff who like kids? |
|---|---|
| Apple | e.g. Can potential customers try our products before buying? |
| Starbucks | e.g. Are we playing really cool music at our shops? |

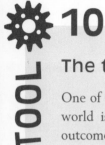

# 10

## The ten-minute brainstorm

One of the best ways for people to survive in a time-poor world is to find ways to achieve the same (or better) outcomes in a shorter time period.

Enter the ten-minute brainstorming session. This is a process whereby participants agree that they must apply maximum creative energy for ten minutes to try to solve a problem.

Here are some guidelines:

- Send out the problem beforehand.

- Ask people to bring along three ideas or images.

- Have each person type the three ideas on a piece of paper and hand a copy to each participant—do not sign the paper (it is anonymous).

- When the meeting starts ask every person to rank the ideas into two categories: 'big ideas' and 'worth exploring further'.

- The group can then use their 120 seconds on the ideas in the 'worth exploring further' category.

- The group can then agree on the top three ideas using a speed evaluation tool (see Chapter 5).

## Application

*The group challenge:* How can we make our brainstorming sessions more productive?

Note: Record the ideas after each minute of interaction.

| Minutes | Ideas developed |
| --- | --- |
| First | Make the sessions shorter. |
| Second | Invite people from outside the group. |
| Third | Start each session with a stirring piece of music. |
| Fourth | Record all the ideas. |
| Fifth | Evaluate the ideas as you go. |
| Sixth | Imagine different perspectives. |
| Seventh | Make it fun. |
| Eighth | Change locations. |
| Ninth | Everyone is given a different role. |
| Tenth | Use some new idea tools. |

'Improvisation works best when everyone is
trying to make everyone else look good.'

Robert Lowe, *Improvisation, Inc.*

# 4

# TEN SPEED THINKING TOOLS TO BUILD A BIGGER IDEA

# The 120-second build

The tools in this chapter will help you to transform a raw idea into a more powerful concept. This is an often neglected stage in the innovation process.

Most people are far too quick to evaluate an idea, and don't give it a chance to grow. This is why these tools have been developed. They will help you to build a bigger, better idea. Creating ideas is the beginning of the creativity process not the end.

The 120-second build is a continuation of the themes of this book. When you are confronted with a problem, someone must start by suggesting a range of possible solutions. You can then take the most attractive of these solutions and in 120 seconds try to build an even stronger idea.

This tool can be used by an individual or with a partner or group.

## Application

*The challenge:* How can we reduce the number of cars on the road?

Take the idea of limiting the number of cars on our streets as a starting point and add nine ways to enhance it.

| 1 Replace cars with motorbikes | 2 Give tax breaks to drivers who give up owning a car | 3 Take it in turns to use the road (odd and even number plates) |
|---|---|---|
| 4 Have bus-only roads | 5 Ban road use at certain times | 6 Give everyone a pushbike |
| 7 Ban large cars | 8 Have weekend drivers' licences | 9 Offer free bus travel |

# The core and nine different executions

A very effective way of thinking about ideas or solutions is to think of every idea as having two dimensions: the core or essence of the idea; and the way the idea has been executed.

Sometimes when we reject an idea we really have a problem with the execution of the idea but the core may still be useful.

For example, think of the core idea of portability. Then recall how many times that core idea has been executed across many different industries or categories. Think of portable sound systems (iPod), portable toilets, portable printers, portable coffee stalls, mobile home mortgage lenders, etc.

Simply separating the core idea from the execution will enable you (or a group) to enhance an existing idea and/or create a new one.

## Application

*The challenge:*

Think of a core idea and play around with as many different approaches to it as you can.

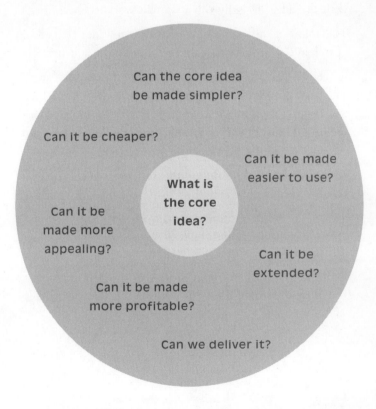

**TOOL**

**3**

## Nine reasons why the idea will work

To make an initial idea bigger will often mean that you will have to change your mindset from 'what is wrong with this idea' to 'why this idea will work'.

This mindset shift almost suggests that any idea regardless of our initial impression can be made bigger and better.

In fact, the history of many ideas is that they started small and grew and grew. For example, Red Nose Day, which was created to increase awareness of sudden infant death syndrome, started off as a small, tentative campaign and grew to become a high-profile, national one.

To use this tool, first define the problem. Then create a number of possible solutions using the Speed Thinking tools in Chapters 1 to 3.

Once you have focused on your high priority ideas then you have another 120 seconds to develop 'how and why' the idea will work.

## Application

***The challenge:*** *How can we increase awareness of the threat of global warming?*

Consider holding a series of suburb by suburb, town hall-type meetings to discuss global warming. Now develop nine reasons why the idea might work.

| | | |
|---|---|---|
| 1 Taps into the local community | 2 Can roll out suburb by suburb | 3 Involve local politicians |
| 4 Develop specific local solutions | 5 People can lead the politicians | 6 People are more engaged when it is close to them |
| 7 Can be tested first | 8 People feel they have a voice | 9 Grass roots democracy |

**TOOL 4**

# Nine reasons why the idea will not work

This tool sounds as if it runs counter to the previous tool. But sometimes there are very good reasons why an idea or a possible new solution may *not* work.

I have found that trying to make these reasons explicit means you can address them and hopefully build a stronger idea.

Identifying the reasons 'why' an idea may not work also means that the people evaluating your idea are forced to articulate their real reasons rather than just saying they do not like it.

This is also a very good tool for anticipating any problems or gaps with your idea. In 120 seconds, ask yourself how and why the idea may not work. After listing these, try to address them before you present your idea. You may have preempted any possible objections and you will gain marks for really thinking through your idea.

## Application

*The challenge:* How can we increase awareness of the threat of global warming?

Again, consider holding a series of suburb by suburb, town hall-type meetings to discuss global warming. Now develop nine reasons why the idea will *not* work.

| | | |
|---|---|---|
| **1** Slow | **2** Expensive | **3** Only so much that local communities can do |
| **4** Louder people can dominate | **5** Avoids a national effort | **6** Can only fit limited numbers in a hall |
| **7** May turn into a talk-fest | **8** People may not turn up | **9** Dominated by politicians |

**TOOL 5**

## Nine quick questions

After you have created your initial or starting idea, a good practice is to ask yourself (or have a colleague ask) nine quick questions about the idea.

The aim with this tool is to develop as many interesting questions you can think of about the idea as fast as you can. Trying to design more original questions might lead you to further explore some part of a possible solution that might otherwise be neglected.

Asking a series of quick questions is important as it enables you to explore and play around with the idea before committing to it one way or another.

To use this tool, first agree upon a challenge. Then in 120 seconds develop a range of new ideas. Then take the three ideas that feel the most attractive and spend another 120 seconds asking as many different questions as you can about each of these.

## Application

*The challenge:* To develop as many interesting questions about the idea as fast as you can.

Ask yourself the following questions quickly and you will end up with a bigger, better idea.

| | | |
|---|---|---|
| 1 What is different about the idea? | 2 What is original about the idea? | 3 What is scary about the idea? |
| 4 Can we test the idea quickly? | 5 Is it a big idea? | 6 Would the competitors hate us doing it? |
| 7 Are we passionate about the idea? | 8 Does the idea move us? | 9 Can we make some money from the idea? |

## Nine different perspectives

Often when you want to create a new idea or solve a problem you tend to look at the issue from one particular view only. This limits your range of options and you may only see a portion of the whole situation.

To create new ideas you need to consider a broader range of perspectives. This shifting from the current lens (L1) to a different lens (L2) is covered in more detail in my book *The Idea Generator*.

Select a problem. In the next 120 seconds write down as many different perspectives from which to view the problem you can think of. Select three at random and consider the view of the situation from this perspective, then use this to make your ideas better. If you are working with a group have everyone in the group adopt one perspective for a few minutes and see what new ideas or insights might emerge.

## Application

*The challenge:* How can we reduce the current level of childhood obesity?

By identifying a range of different perspectives you will be in a better position to create a pool of more original ideas. The problem can be viewed, for example, from the perspectives of those listed below.

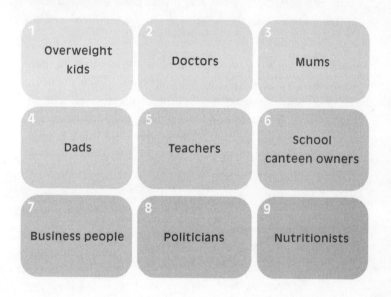

**TOOL 7**

## Random build

The usual way to build an idea is to do so in a logical and deliberate manner. By doing so you tend to use your rational, conscious mind and hence any further ideas tend to be incremental and safe.

But, as Edward De Bono and others have suggested, our mind acts as a patterning system from which we need to deliberately break free.[1]

This can be achieved by being more random in our thinking. For example, select a problem. Then create a range of new ideas quickly using the 120-second guidelines. Target one idea at random—the fifth one, for example. Then build nine new ways of making the idea better. Again at random select a few of these and really develop them further.

Using this random process might lead to occasional waste but it can unlock a truly original and breakthrough idea.

## Application

*The challenge:* How can we acquire new customers when we have a limited budget?

Create lots of ideas as fast as you can. Then select a range of these at random (for example 3, 5, 7 below) and really develop these. You might create a big, new concept.

| | | |
|---|---|---|
| 1 Encourage word of mouth | 2 Use email | 3 Try to partner with another company |
| 4 Approach the government | 5 Ask your current customers for leads | 6 Network |
| 7 Share customers with others | 8 Generate PR | 9 Surprise your customer |

# TOOL 8

## The power of two (in half the time)

Your role with this tool is to make the idea in front of you twice as powerful. This is a very good tool to use with a partner or group.

The challenge is set and the ideas are created. As a suggestion use the 120-second Speed Thinking template (see Chapter 2, Speed Thinking Tool 1) to create at least nine ideas.

Then select one idea, or if you are working in a group give each idea to one person. Their challenge is to take this starting idea and try to make it twice as powerful. Then you can evaluate all the ideas knowing that you have really tried to explore the latent potential of each idea.

This is a very powerful tool as it pushes the person reviewing the idea to be as creative as they possibly can. The idea thus becomes not 'my' idea but 'our' idea.

## Application

*The challenge:* How can we engage students in the political process?

**The starting idea:** Have a school-wide essay competition

**Ways to make this idea twice as powerful:**

- Run separate private vs public school competitions

- The winners present their ideas to the prime minister

- The ideas are submitted on a website and the public can vote on the winner

## TOOL 9

### The 120-second block

If you are working in a group and someone raises an obstacle to an idea, set a challenge between the different members to see who can be the first to find a way to overcome the obstacle. Find nine ways to overcome this obstacle in 120 seconds.

The person who has the best response could win a chocolate, for example.

If you are working by yourself and you have reached an obstacle to your idea try to develop at least nine ways of overcoming the objection.

This will encourage you to explore different solutions and to really think through the idea.

## Application

*The challenge:* To generate more business in a café.

| The starting idea | The blockages | How can we overcome them? |
|---|---|---|
| e.g. Offer a free coffee with every meal. | Costly. | Still charge for the coffee but offer a free one when the customer returns (i.e. encourage repeat business). |

## 10

TOOL

## Idea to concept in express time

Creating new ideas is only one third of the job. The next stage is to transform these ideas into workable concepts. The last phase is to test your concepts.

For many people, transforming a starting idea into a concept is difficult. That is why I have developed the questions opposite to help you.

Once you have created a new idea, work your way through the various questions until you have designed a bigger concept. If you find that you are having trouble answering the questions then it may mean you have to go back to the drawing board and develop a new range of ideas.

It is important in this stage not to become obsessed with an idea. Passion is important but if the idea cannot be transformed into a workable concept then let it go. It may not be the right time, and other ideas may be more productive.

## Application

*The challenge:* To build a powerful new concept from your starting idea.

Take your starting idea and spend 120 seconds on each of the stages outlined below—in 12 minutes you can build a powerful new concept.

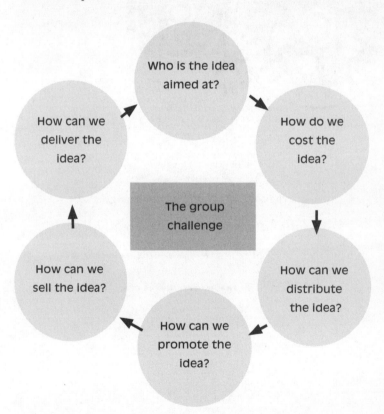

'I find more reasons to do things than
not to do them. My motto really is:
"Screw it—let's do it".'

Richard Branson, *Screw it, Let's Do It*

# 5

## TEN SPEED THINKING TOOLS TO HELP EVALUATE AN IDEA

**TOOL**

**1**

## The 120-second priority

Try to make people evaluate their ideas quickly. Give them at most 120 seconds to decide on the best ideas.

This is one way to ensure that you use your intuition rather than your rational, conscious mind. Sometimes an idea just 'feels right' and this feeling needs to be respected.

I have found that if you give people too much time they tend to over-analyse the idea and shift into a judgement mode, which means that most ideas are dismissed and the most original ideas barely rate a mention.

The other benefit of giving people only a short period of time to judge an idea is that they are less influenced by what others are saying as they are too busy evaluating their own ideas.

## Application

When you are evaluating an idea select the top five ideas and provide a one-word rationale as to why you selected the idea e.g. different, engaging, challenging, cheaper. Evaluate all the ideas in 120 seconds.

**First choice:**

**Second choice:**

**Third choice:**

**Fourth choice:**

**Fifth choice:**

**TOOL 2**

## The evaluation race

This is an extension of the first tool. Often our 'gut feeling' is the best indicator of whether or not an idea has merit.

However, because most of us have been taught to consider all the alternatives and carefully and prudently consider a cost–benefit of all the possible options, we often have trouble making up our mind.

The other problem in evaluating ideas is that we are often influenced by the reactions of others. If everyone else thinks it is a good idea then often it takes a brave person to go against the crowd.

One way around these two problems is to have an evaluation race. Everyone in the group is competing to evaluate all the ideas as quickly as possible. Each person is given three ticks that they can spread across all the ideas as they see fit. The best ideas are the ones that score highest according to the number of ticks each idea receives.

This tool makes the evaluation process fun and highly individual.

## Application

Evaluate all the ideas as quickly as you can. The first person in a group to do so wins a prize (it could be a chocolate bar, for example).

| Highest scoring ideas: | |
| --- | --- |
| Average scoring ideas: | |
| Lowest scoring ideas: | |

## The scariest ideas

When I am running workshops on Speed Thinking one of the most effective ways participants have found to evaluate an idea is to select those ideas that are the scariest.

The word choice is important. I do not say 'evaluate the ideas that are the wildest or most different'. By asking for the scariest ideas you are asking people to select the ideas that elicit a definite emotion, particularly if this is done quickly.

When you or a group select the scariest ideas ask yourself the following questions:

- What makes this idea so scary? Is it because it is so original and so different from what we have tried before?
- Is there a way we can reduce the risk?
- How can we test this idea, or a version of it, quickly, easily and cheaply?

## Application

When you are evaluating an idea, select the top ideas based on the degree to which the idea makes you feel uncomfortable or is downright scary. Evaluate the ideas in 120 seconds.

| Scariest idea: | |
|---|---|
| Still scary: | |
| A bit scary: | |
| Hardly scary at all: | |
| Quite tame: | |

**4**

**TOOL**

## Ten dollars to invest

I have found this to be a very good tool to help people evaluate an idea. Start by giving each person in the group $10 (in $1 coins) and let them know they can evaluate an idea by investing in the ideas that will give the greatest return. Each person must evaluate all the ideas on the table in 120 seconds so that you rely on your intuition and imagination.

There is something about giving people real money that makes the meeting more focused and tends to make decisions between ideas easier.

Another variation on this is to ask people the question: 'If this was your business, which ideas would you support?'

Giving people money is also a dramatic and symbolic way of highlighting that ideas are vital to the continued financial health of an organisation.

## Application

You have $10 each to invest in up to four ideas. You can invest as much as you want in any of the top four ideas. The top idea could get the entire amount if you feel that passionate about it. Allocate your amount in the next 120 seconds.

| The idea description: | Amount invested: |
|---|---|
|  |  |
|  |  |
|  |  |
|  |  |

Total: $10

**5**

## The judges panel

Have you ever watched an event at the Olympics, such as diving or gymnastics? The athletes perform and the judges must score the performance, almost immediately, out of ten.

This tool works on exactly the same principle. The judges must make an assessment based on set criteria and according to their best judgement.

Decide in advance how an idea is to be evaluated. You could decide to award a maximum of five points for originality and five points for impact. When you are shown an idea then you must give it a score *immediately* based on the two criteria.

This is a fun tool to use in a group as you can rotate the judging panel, no one person can dominate the scores and there are always other judges.

The other benefit of this approach is that the results can be made transparent so you can see exactly how each judge votes.

## Application

Agree upon the criteria all judges must use to evaluate an idea. Then select a panel and give each judge a set of large cards with the numbers one to ten on them (if ten is the maximum score).

After an idea has been presented, ask each judge to hold up a card with their score on it.

The ideas with the highest scores are the winners.

A variation of this might be for the judges to score the ideas on the basis of how uncomfortable or scary they find the idea (see Speed Thinking Tool 3 in this chapter).

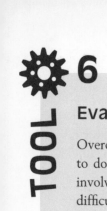

## Evaluate on passion only

Overcoming inertia in an organisation is a difficult thing to do at the best of times. But when an idea is new and involves a significant change then it becomes even more difficult.

An idea can be evaluated according to how much money it might make or how strategically important it might be. These are worthwhile and sensible criteria. However, I have run many workshops where group members have voted on a particular idea as being the highest scoring and when I have asked who wants to work on it not a hand goes up!

Ideas need to be evaluated on reason (head) and passion (heart). That is why it is a good practice to ask people how they might rate an idea on the basis of how passionate they feel about the idea. With passion a committed group can move mountains; without it an idea will not move.

## Application

When you are evaluating a set of ideas, select the top ideas based on your level of passion for the idea, regardless of any other consideration. Evaluate the ideas in 120 seconds.

| Ideas that I am extremely passionate about: | |
|---|---|
| Ideas that I am reasonably passionate about: | |
| Ideas that I have some passion for: | |
| Ideas I feel indifferent about: | |
| Ideas that I have no passion for: | |

## TOOL 7

### Decimal points

When evaluating an idea, try to consider the number of dollar decimal points an idea might return.

For example, ask yourself, 'Will this idea generate a return of two decimal places (hundreds of dollars) or three (thousands of dollars) or four (tens of thousands)?'

This approach will give you a quick feel for the size of the idea.

If you are working in a group have every person independently score the return on an idea. Then place people together who have a major variance in how they scored the idea. For example, one person might score the return in the hundreds of dollars and another person in the tens of thousands. This variation is worth discussing and often provides the magic in the evaluation process.

## Application

When you are evaluating an idea, quickly assess whether the idea can have a two-, three- or four-figure impact. Rely on your gut feeling; you do not have to justify your decision.

| | |
|---|---|
| Ideas with four-figure impact: | |
| Ideas with three-figure impact: | |
| Ideas with two-figure impact: | |

**TOOL**

# 8

## The quick balance sheet

A very simple and quick way of evaluating an idea is to use a balance sheet-type approach. Quickly list all the pros of the idea and then the cons.

At this early stage it is important not to order the pros or cons, simply list these.

The next stage is to order the top three pros and the top three cons.

Finally, spend another 120 seconds on trying to overcome each con and then another 120 seconds on how to enhance each pro of the idea.

When you have finished this exercise, re-evaluate the idea.

## Application

Spend 120 seconds writing down the pros and cons of each idea.

If you are working in a group, give each group member a number of ideas at random. They will write down the pros and cons of these ideas and at the end of this process you will be in a better position to evaluate each idea.

| Pros of the idea | Cons of the idea |
| --- | --- |
| e.g. Different to what we have done in the past | e.g. Sounds expensive |

**TOOL 9**

# Evaluate according to potential impact and time to market

When people evaluate an idea, they often do this in isolation from other ideas. This approach has the benefit of each idea being treated on its merits.

However, ideas, projects or solutions often emerge in clusters and most compete with each other for scarce resources. That is why I like to use a grid-type approach (see the application opposite).

On one axis you have potential impact (or sales/revenue) and on the other is time to market (or ease of implementation). Using these two axes you can place each project or solution on the grid. The benefit of this approach is that you can not only place each idea but see where it fits with other ideas.

This visual picture allows the group to see where the ideas are located. It may well be that all the ideas are wonderful but have long-term time frames. The group could then ask what they could achieve in the short term.

This is an ideal tool to do quickly as you just want to get a feel for the ideas and where they sit in relation to each other.

## Application

The team has to discuss each idea or project in 120 seconds and agree where it should fit on the grid below, which measures time to market (horizontal axis) and potential impact, e.g. revenue, sales (vertical axis).

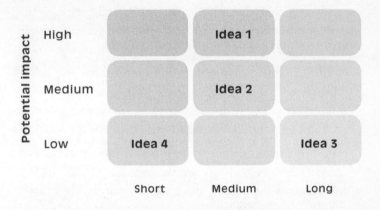

# 10

## Nine reasons to say yes

This is a very good tool to use when you have culled a large number of ideas down to a short list of, say, half a dozen.

With this short list it is important to fully explore the potential of every idea. As a result it makes sense to reverse the usual tendency of saying no to most ideas to outlining reasons to say yes.

The Speed Thinking approach is ideal because it enables you to come up with many reasons to say yes to every idea in the priority list in a short period of time.

After you have completed this, revisit the short list and decide which ideas really are the top ones. Select the top idea that might possess the most yes votes or the most convincing case for yes votes.

## Application

Decide to use word of mouth to attract talented, new people to your business. Now find nine reasons to say yes to this idea:

| | | |
|---|---|---|
| **1** Save money | **2** Like-minded people | **3** More credible |
| **4** Quality not quantity | **5** Can pay more as you are not wasting money on job ads | **6** Feels special |
| **7** Steady stream | **8** Encourages existing staff to look for talent | **9** Will be talked about |

'To start is the fundamental
creative act.'

Michael Hewitt-Gleeson, *Software for the Brain 2*

# 6 TEN SPEED THINKING TOOLS TO GET STARTED

## TOOL

# 1

## Five-minute 'gut feel' time

In most work situations you are expected to act in a logical and rational manner. This is particularly true when you are in a meeting or a presentation.

Yet with this dominance of reason there often exists little time for your intuition to emerge. The irony is that your intuition informs most of your decisions. But it is rarely acknowledged or discussed.

One way to overcome this—and to ultimately make better decisions—is to dedicate five minutes in every meeting to intuition or 'gut feeling'. This is a very powerful process, particularly when you have just made a decision. After a decision has been made, ask the group what their 'gut feeling' is. It is important to stress that people are free to talk about their intuition without needing to support or verify it.

People who have used this process are amazed at the energy that is released in the group. Group members often say 'the numbers don't add up but my gut feeling is that this is still a good idea' or something similar.

The advantage of this approach is that these feelings are out in the open and can be discussed rather than remain hidden. It is also important that the group leader should highlight that no 'gut-feel' comment is to be sneered at or criticised.

# Application

*The challenge: Should we hire this new person for our business?*

| The initial decision: | e.g. Yes, because they have all the necessary experience and qualifications. |
|---|---|
| 'Gut feel' discussion: | e.g. But do not feel they will fit into our culture. |
| The final decision: | e.g. We should keep looking. |

## 2

### The ten-minute walk

According to many writers the creative process consists of a number of stages. Perhaps the most famous was developed by Graham Wallas.[1] He suggested that the four key stages were:

1. Preparation: gathering all the relevant information on the problem at hand.

2. Incubation: allowing the problem to be mulled over in the mind.

3. Illumination: the 'aha!' moment.

4. Verification: testing whether the new ideas can be implemented.

These four steps seem to resonate with most people. But why wait for the mind to create a new idea? Sometimes the simple act of letting go of the problem and going for a ten-minute walk can fast-track a new solution.

The other benefit is that you will get some exercise. I have found that working on two problems at once can lead to a cross-fertilisation of ideas. In either case you are working in a faster and more productive manner.

## Application

*The challenge:* How can I find an exciting new job?

| | |
|---|---|
| The relevant information I need: | e.g. Visit job-search websites for similar positions. |
| Ideas from the ten-minute incubation walk: | e.g. But what do I feel really passionate about? |
| The solution: | e.g. Broaden my search criteria to include roles that I know I will enjoy. |
| How to verify: | e.g. Talk to people outside my role about what they like about their job. |

## Nine high-impact actions

One of the most effective ways to improve your performance quickly is to think in terms of five-day blocks. Ask yourself: What potentially high-impact actions can I take this week?

This type of thinking will focus your energy on making a big impact very quickly. This may not be sustainable over a year but you may, for example, have an intensive five-day block followed by a slower paced one. This type of approach is similar to how athletes prepare for an upcoming event with very high-load training weeks before an event, followed by a tapering-off period.

With a Speed Thinking approach you can control the pace at which you think and act. It does not have to be at the same pace. When the situation demands it, you can increase it and then slow it down when things quieten down.

## Application

**The challenge:** *How can I generate an increase in sales and cash flow quickly?*

| | | |
|---|---|---|
| **1** Make three new new business calls a day | **2** Ring accounts receivable every day | **3** Offer a money-back guarantee on new business |
| **4** Provide a 20% discount if people pay quickly | **5** Focus on my top three potential clients | **6** Create some PR |
| **7** Offer a $500 'get a new customer' program | **8** Send a gift to the accounts receivable staff | **9** Go back to my existing clients |

**TOOL 4**

## Three things to test today

I believe that every manager or leader should be testing three new things every day. They do not have to be big things but you need to be constantly pushing the envelope. It could be having a shorter meeting, encouraging staff to use a Speed Thinking tool or meeting a new customer. Whatever it is, write down in the next 120 seconds three things you want to test.

It matters little *what* is being tested. What is important is that you are building a test or experimental mindset. This approach ensures that you try new ideas (after all, it is only a test) and you become very action oriented. It also ensures that you are continually growing as a person and as a leader.

The important part of a daily testing mindset is that you need to test things quickly, easily and cheaply. This will involve creativity and the Speed Thinking approach is ideal for creating new ways of testing your three daily priorities.

## Application

*The challenge:* How can I improve my health today?

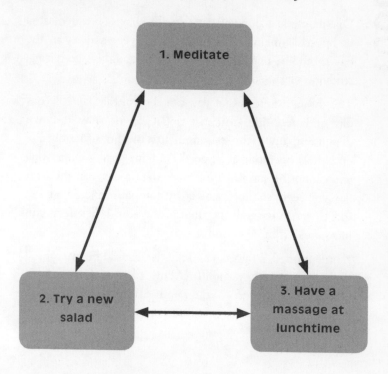

Pick one and test it today.

**TOOL**

# 5

## A Speed Thinking day

One dramatic action you can take is to have a day dedicated to Speed Thinking. This means that every activity in the day should be done at a faster pace. It could be exercising, studying or thinking.

The thought here is that you can control the pace of your day and your life. You can rev it up or slow it down depending upon the requirements of the situation. An entire day operating at a Speed Thinking pace is exhausting and cannot be sustained for more than a day. But the next day will seem so much slower by comparison and you will feel that you have all the time in the world. In effect, you have created more time for yourself.

As mentioned, a Speed Thinking day should be attempted perhaps once every month. Allow plenty of time both before and after for your body, mind and spirit to recover.

# Application

*The challenge:* To spend the entire day at an accelerated thinking pace and record the results.

| Activity: | Results: |
| --- | --- |
| e.g. I listened to and expressed my 'gut feeling' in a meeting. | Many other group members had the same feeling I did. |

How does it compare with a usual day?

6

## My nine lessons learned this week

One of the false impressions of Speed Thinking is that it is about mindless actions. Nothing could be further from the truth. Speed Thinking is a way of unlocking the creative potential of your subconscious.

The same process can be used to reflect upon your actions this week. If you can continuously learn every week then you will grow as a person and, for example, as a manager if you work in business.

One way to do this is at the end of the week, say Friday lunchtime, write down in 120 seconds the nine lessons you have learned and what you may do differently in the future.

This approach to Speed Thinking and learning will quicken your development and give you an edge over others as they are trapped either by indecision and/or repeating the mistakes of the past.

## Application

**The challenge:** *How can I improve my work/life balance?*

| 1 Practise my Speed Thinking | 2 Ask my current clients for referrals | 3 Create more P.R. |
|---|---|---|
| 4 Watch my weight | 5 Practise my kung-fu | 6 Ask my daughter more specific questions |
| 7 Love my kids | 8 Keep early mornings free | 9 Have fun |

7

TOOL

## Nine uncomfortable actions

Most of us like to lead a comfortable life. By this I do not only mean financially or materially comfortable. This is desirable but does not guarantee happiness. We also strive to be emotionally comfortable. On the positive side this can mean that we have developed happy and stable relationships with others and are reasonably accepting of ourselves. However, being too comfortable can also mean we can become rigid and narrow. It might mean, for example, that you are unwilling to take new risks or try anything new.

To overcome this mindset I suggest you use the Speed Thinking approach to write down nine uncomfortable actions you can take in the next nine days. Don't analyse, just write them down in a hurry and see what happens. The actions could be physical, emotional or spiritual. Pushing ourselves out of our comfort zones is a liberating process.

## Application

*The challenge:* How can I push myself out of my comfort zone?

| | | |
|---|---|---|
| 1 Make more cold calls | 2 Follow up more | 3 Go to the gym every day |
| 4 Ring previous business partner | 5 Go back to previous clients | 6 Start every meeting on time |
| 7 Dress up for business meetings | 8 Do canteen duty at son's/daughter's school | 9 Read a magazine that I would not normally read |

## TOOL 8

## Meetings in half the time

For many people, both in business and life generally, meetings are the bane of their existence. There are far too many and not much seems to get done. As a result meetings are becoming more formalised, with rigid agendas to ensure that meetings start and end on time.

These formal incremental strategies rarely seem to work. What is needed is a far more radical approach. You should set yourself the challenge of having your next meeting in half the usual time while still expecting to achieve the same outcomes.

This big, hairy goal can only be achieved by thinking and acting in a Speed Thinking way. You will find, paradoxically, that more gets done. Better decisions are made as more options are considered and people feel more energised.

Imagine the productivity in the organisation if the length of every meeting could be reduced by half? Every employee could then return to their usual role and have more time up their sleeve to reach their goals or offer better service to a customer.

## Application

**The challenge:** *To come up with nine ways to have a quicker and more effective meeting.*

| | | |
|---|---|---|
| 1 Send an agenda out before the meeting | 2 Bring three ideas already prepared | 3 Set a time limit |
| 4 Have shorter meetings more often | 5 Only meet every second day | 6 Don't meet in the morning |
| 7 Ask if the meeting is necessary | 8 Rotate the Chair | 9 Start on time |

## Nine ways to practise Speed Thinking

Speed thinking, like any skill, needs to be practised if you are to improve at it. But unlike most activities it does not need an expensive range of equipment. For the price of this book you will have all the starting equipment and tools you need.

In learning how to improve your Speed Thinking, start slowly. Tackle problems that are easy and most of all enjoy the process. For example, what are nine different ways you could have travelled to work this morning? You could have walked, caught a train, hitchhiked, etc.

The moment that you feel too much pressure, scale it back. The aim is to consistently reach nine new possibilities in 120 seconds for most problems.

I have listed nine ways to practise Speed Thinking on the opposite page. Enjoy yourself as you start to experience the power of your own imagination to solve problems quickly and easily.

## Application

***The challenge:*** *How can I practise Speed Thinking?*

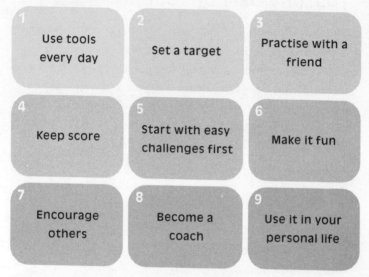

| | | |
|---|---|---|
| 1 Use tools every day | 2 Set a target | 3 Practise with a friend |
| 4 Keep score | 5 Start with easy challenges first | 6 Make it fun |
| 7 Encourage others | 8 Become a coach | 9 Use it in your personal life |

You can visit **www.thespeedthinkingzone.com** for the latest news and tips.

## 10

**TOOL**

### Nine ways to make Speed Thinking part of your life

The entire purpose of this book is to help you think and act in a faster and more productive way. This will enable you to achieve more and ease your stress as you will rarely feel under time pressure again. If anything, having a shorter period of time in which to come up with ideas or solutions will force you to unlock your subconscious mind, which seems to be wired to work at a faster pace.

As with any other skill, to achieve a level of proficiency in Speed Thinking requires that you start to embed it in your life.

I have listed a range of possible actions you can use. The list is not exhaustive and you can create and build your own list in the next 120 seconds.

Speed Thinking is not the only type of thinking but it will enhance and simplify your life.

Think quickly. You do not have two minutes to waste.

## Application

***The challenge:*** *How can I practise Speed Thinking more often?*

| | | |
|---|---|---|
| 1 Develop a Speed Thinker's diary | 2 Send myself a reminder to use it every day | 3 Talk to others about the concept |
| 4 Never turn down an opportunity to use it | 5 Run a group using it | 6 Surround myself with other Speed Thinkers |
| 7 Have Speed Thinking competitions | 8 Form a Speed Thinker's network | 9 Practise every day |

# CONCLUSION

## The most commonly asked questions about Speed Thinking

### What is Speed Thinking?

It is a way of thinking where we accelerate the normal pace at which we might create new ideas, think of new solutions and make decisions. It is a way of accessing the creative potential of our imagination and intuition.

### How and why does it work?

We all have two judges who can interfere with the originality and freshness of our own ideas. The first is our internal judge, who often reminds us of everything we cannot do. This is the cautious voice inside our head that tries to stop us appearing foolish and aims to protect our self-esteem.

The second judge is the external one. It relates to our friends, peers, colleagues and bosses, who can be very quick to find fault with our ideas.

These two judges, one internal and one external, combine to limit the power of our thinking and therefore our ability to solve problems in novel ways. The use of Speed Thinking tends to bypass these two judges as the subconscious mind steps in and produces a range of often powerful new solutions.

## How does Speed Thinking compare with traditional thinking?

Our usual way of thinking is based on careful analysis, logic and reason.

However, the world seems to be moving at an ever-increasing pace and this type of thinking often struggles with the pace of change that is required to cope. Traditional thinking is predicated on having sufficient and timely information to make decisions. Again, this is not always possible in many situations.

Speed Thinking can provide a more appropriate way of dealing with the pace of change and limited information. It complements and enhances traditional thinking.

It is also a very effective way of unlocking the more imaginative parts of your mind which complement the more rational, analytical modes of thinking.

## Can anyone learn Speed Thinking?

Yes. This type of thinking is a way of tapping into an ability that is present in all of us. It is the same skill that enables experts to make rapid, life and death decisions in emergencies, for example.

Based on my experience, some people are better at it than others but it is a skill that can be learned and improved with practice. Certainly some people seem to be more open and responsive than others but this is always the challenge when you are trying something new.

The tools in this book provide a practical way for most people to improve their Speed Thinking results.

## Can you use it all the time?

Speed Thinking can be applied to most types of everyday problems and decisions. It is particularly useful when you require new approaches or when you feel stuck. Speed Thinking provides a burst of thinking energy and can be used regularly depending upon the need. It is a bit like speed chess, for example, in that you may not have the time for a full game but you might have time for a quick one. And, like speed chess, the nature of Speed Thinking is slightly different from, but complementary to, traditional thinking.

## Why 120 seconds and nine responses?

There is nothing hard and fast about taking 120 seconds and achieving nine responses. It was arrived at by trial and error in my workshops. I found that nine responses ensured that people were sufficiently challenged and very focused. About one third of people achieve the goal. But the rest of the group can usually create between five and eight responses, which provides a reachable platform to move to the higher goal. The figure nine is also consistent with the finding that our short-term memory can handle seven plus or minus two items at any one point in time.

## Are there some circumstances in which Speed Thinking is more productive?

Yes. Teresa Amabile (among others) is a Harvard professor who has spent considerable time studying the effects of time pressure and creativity. Her findings suggest that 'creative thinking under extreme pressure is more likely when people feel they are on a mission and they can stay focused on one activity without distraction'.[1] She does warn, however, that high levels of time pressure cannot be sustained for long periods without a break. I agree with her, which is why I suggest Speed Thinking be used in short, regular spells, much like skipping or boxing within an overall fitness program. It is something that can be used every day to unlock new ideas and give you an energy boost.

# NOTES

## Introduction

1. M. Gladwell, *Blink: The power of thinking without thinking*, Penguin, Melbourne, 2005, p. 50.
2. For a wonderful read on the power of our intuition see, G. Klein, *The Power of Intuition: How to use your gut feelings to make better decisions at work*, Random House, New York, 2004.
3. T.D. Wilson, *Strangers to Ourselves: Discovering the adaptive unconscious*, Harvard University Press, Cambridge, 2002, p. 35.
4. W. Gallwey, *The Inner Game of Tennis*, Pan Books, London, 1972, pp. 32–4.
5. D. Nason, 'A-Rod's April batting feats help to subdue the steroid rage', *Australian*, 26 April 2007, p. 35.
6. E. Pronin and Daniel Wegner, 'Manic Thinking: Independent effects of thought speed and thought content on mood', *Psychological Science*, 17(9), September 2006, pp. 807–13.
7. K. Blanchard and S. Johnson, *The One Minute Manager*, HarperCollins, London, 1981, Chapter 1.

## Chapter 1

1. This is an adaptation of Edward De Bono's Random Word technique: see E. De Bono, *Sur/Petition: Going beyond competition*, HarperCollins, London, 1992, pp. 183–5.

## Chapter 3

1. T. Buzan, *Make the Most of Your Mind*, Simon & Schuster, London, 1988, p. 117.

## Chapter 4

1. E. De Bono, *Serious Creativity: Using the power of lateral thinking to create new ideas*, HarperCollins, London, 1992, pp. 8–17.

## Chapter 6

1. G. Wallas, *The Art of Thought*, Wiley & Sons, New York, 1926.

## Conclusion

1. T.M. Amabile, C.N. Hadley and S.J. Kramer, 'Creativity under the gun', *Harvard Business Review*, August, 2002, pp. 52–61.

# FURTHER READING

Blanchard K. and Johnson, S., *The One Minute Manager*, HarperCollins, 1981.

Buzan T., *Make the Most of Your Mind*, Simon & Schuster, 1988.

De Bono E., *Serious Creativity: Using the power of lateral thinking to create new ideas*, HarperCollins, 1992.

Gladwell M., *Blink: The power of thinking without thinking*, Penguin Books, 2005.

Hudson, K., *The Idea Generator*, Allen & Unwin, 2007.

Kawashima, R., *Train Your Brain*, Penguin Books, 2007.

Klein, G., *The Power of Intuition: How to make better decisions at work*, Random House, 2004.

Wilson, T.D., *Strangers to Ourselves: Discovering the adaptive unconscious*, Harvard University Press, 2002.

## NOTES

# NOTES

**NOTES**

# NOTES

NOTES

# NOTES

## NOTES